# CLASSIC PUDS

...it's SO economical !

# CLASSIC
## *Australian*
# PUDS

### *From Pavlovas to Trifles*
### ALICE MAY

ALLEN & UNWIN

First published in 1993 by
Allen & Unwin
9 Atchison Street
St Leonards NSW 2065
Australia

Created and produced by
Modern Times Pty Ltd
P.O. Box 908
Bondi Junction NSW 2022,
Australia

National Library of Australia
Cataloguing-in-Publication entry:

May, Alice L.
        Classic Australian puds.

        Includes index.
        ISBN 1 86373 546 1.

        1. Puddings. 2. Cookery (Puddings). 3. Cookery, Australian. I. Title.

641.8640994

Produced by Mandarin Offset, Hong Kong

# CONTENTS

# INTRODUCTION

O<small>NCE UPON</small> a time the kitchen was the centre of life. It was a place from which the family was nourished - both literally and figuratively; where food was stored, meals prepared and families gathered. The kitchen was by inclination a casual place and the hub of many activities. There were puddings to make and fruit to stew, jam to boil and pies to bake. The table was filled daily with home produced delights - and we always wanted more. This was when our mothers or grandmothers cooked and baked every meal and we ate at home and loved it. C<small>LASSIC</small> P<small>UDS</small> recalls those days with nostalgia and sentiment.

## APPLE CHARLOTTE

*100 g (4 oz) breadcrumbs*
*grated rind of 1 lemon*
*pinch of cinnamon*
*100 g (4 oz) sugar*
*juice of 1 lemon*
*60 g (2 ½ oz) butter*
*5 large cooking apples, peeled, cored and sliced*

P REHEAT oven to 180 deg C (350 deg F). Grease a large ovenproof dish generously with butter. Mix together the breadcrumbs, grated lemon rind, cinnamon and sugar. Line the bottom of the prepared dish with one-third of the breadcrumb mixture. Pour a little lemon juice over the breadcrumbs and dot with butter. Place a layer of half the apples over the breadcrumbs. Repeat a layer of breadcrumbs and another layer of apples. Finish with a layer of breadcrumbs. Pour over a little lemon juice and dot with butter. Bake for 1 ¼ hrs

*Don't put sliced apples into cold water to preserve their whiteness; it decreases their flavour.*

## APPLE PIE

*1 quantity rich shortcrust pastry (see Rich
Shortcrust Pastry recipe)
7 green cooking apples, peeled, cored and sliced thinly
185 g (6 ½ oz) sugar
1 tablespoon plain (all-purpose) flour
1 teaspoon ground cinnamon
pinch of grated nutmeg
pinch of salt
25 g (1 oz) butter
egg white, slightly beaten
sugar, extra*

P REHEAT oven to 200 deg C (400 deg F). Grease a pie dish
with butter. Roll out two-thirds of pastry on a lightly
floured surface and line the prepared dish. Mix in a bowl the
sliced apple, sugar, flour, cinnamon, nutmeg and salt. Spoon
into the prepared pastry and dot with butter. Roll out remaining
pastry to cover the pie.

Trim off excess pastry and crimp the edges. With any leftover pieces of pastry make leaf shapes to decorate pie top. Brush with beaten egg white to glaze. Make two or three steam vents and sprinkle lightly with sugar. Bake for 1 to 1 ¼ hours. Reduce the heat if the pastry is becoming too brown.

### APPLE SNOW

*250 g (9 oz) sieved cooked apple*
*150 g (5 oz) caster (superfine) sugar*
*Juice of ½ lemon*
*4 egg whites*
*pinch of salt*

PREHEAT oven to 180 deg C (350 deg F). Grease a shallow ovenproof dish lightly with butter. Put the apple pulp in a bowl and stir in the sugar and lemon juice. Beat the egg whites with the salt until stiff peaks form. Fold into the apple mixture. Spoon into the prepared dish and lightly brown in the oven.

## APPLE SPONGE PUDDING

*125 g (4 ½ oz) plain (all-purpose) flour*
*1 level teaspoon baking powder*
*1 tablespoon butter*
*125 g (4 ½ oz) sugar*
*1 egg*
*milk*
*600 ml (20 fl oz) cooked apples (or other cooked fruit)*

PREHEAT oven to 160 deg C (325 deg F). Grease an ovenproof dish generously with butter. Sift the flour with the baking powder.

Beat the butter and sugar until creamy, light and fluffy. Add the egg, beating very well. Gently fold the sifted flour into the creamed mixture. Add enough milk to make a stiff batter. Pour the stewed apples into the base of the prepared dish. Spoon the batter over the apples. Bake until golden brown.

*Before heating milk rinse the saucepan with cold water
and it will not scorch so easily.*

## BREAD AND BUTTER CUSTARD

*200g (7 oz) fresh, sliced, white bread, crusts removed
butter
150 g (5 oz) mixed dried fruit
vanilla
3 eggs
2 egg yolks
125 g (4 ½ oz) sugar
500 ml (17 fl oz) milk*

PREHEAT oven to 200 deg C (400 deg F). Grease a pie or ovenproof dish lightly with butter. Butter the bread slices and brown under a grill. Cut the slices into triangles, and arrange an overlapping layer of bread on the base of the dish. Sprinkle with dried fruit. Place another layer over this and sprinkle again with dried fruit.

Beat eggs and yolks with sugar until the mixture is well combined. Heat the milk and remove from heat. Add to the mixture, stirring well. Pour mixture over the bread and fruit that is in the prepared dish. Place dish in a larger baking pan, pour enough water in the larger pan to come halfway up the sides of the dish. Bake for 30 minutes or until custard has set.

## CASTLE PUDDINGS

*185 g (6 ½ oz) plain (all-purpose) flour*
*1/2 teaspoon bicarbonate of soda (baking soda)*
*1 teaspoon cream of tartar*
*2 tablespoons butter*
*125 g (4 ½ oz) sugar*
*2 eggs*
*125 ml (4 ½ fl oz) milk*
*currants*

P REHEAT oven to 180 deg C (350 deg F). Grease small soufflé dishes generously with butter and sprinkle bases with a few currants. Sift the flour with the bicarbonate of soda and cream of tartar.

Beat the butter and sugar until creamy, light and fluffy. Add the eggs one at a time, beating very well after each one is added. Gently fold the sifted flour into the creamed mixture alternately with the milk. Spoon the mixture into the prepared dishes. The mixture should half-fill the dishes. Bake for about 20 minutes until well risen.

BRISK LIPTON TEA
REVIVES YOU FAST!

## CHARLOTTE RUSSE

*1 packet of 24 Savoiardi fingers,*
*sponge finger or lady finger biscuits*
*5 g ( ¼ oz) gelatine*
*2 tablespoons water*
*2 tablespoons milk*
*300 ml (10 fl oz) cream*
*½ to 1 teaspoon vanilla (or brandy)*
*35 g (1 ½ oz) caster (superfine) sugar*
*150 ml (5 fl oz) lemon jelly*

L INE THE base and sides of a 23 cm (9 in) springform pan with the sponge fingers. Trim the tops and sides so that they fit snugly together and are not too tall.

Over a gentle heat dissolve the gelatine in the water. Stir in the milk. Beat the cream until light and fluffy. Stir the gelatine, vanilla or brandy and sugar into the cream. Combine well. Pour into the prepared pan. Refrigerate until set.

Pour a thin layer of cool liquid lemon jelly over the top of the filling and refrigerate until set. Remove pan and decorate with whipped cream.

## CHOCOLATE BLANC MANGE

*3 heaped dessertspoons cornflour (cornstarch)*
*3 heaped teaspoons cocoa powder*
*3 heaped dessertspoons sugar*
*750 ml (25 fl oz) milk*
*vanilla*

S TIR together the cornflour, cocoa powder, sugar and enough of the cold milk to make a runny mixture. Mix until smooth. Put remaining milk in a saucepan and heat gently, do not boil. Stirring vigorously, add the cocoa mixture. Stir until fully incorporated and mixture begins to simmer. Pour into a dish or bowl and chill.

*Whenever a recipe says "Gelatine" — it means Davis Gelatine.*

# DAVIS GELATINE

*To blanch almonds pour boiling water over them.*
*Allow them to stand in the water for a few minutes*
*and then lift them out and remove their skins.*
*Almonds that are freshly peeled*
*have more flavour.*

## CHRISTMAS PUDDING

225 g (8 oz) plain (all-purpose) flour
pinch of salt
½ teaspoon mixed spice
225 g (8 oz) butter
225 g (8 oz) brown sugar
5 eggs
100 g (4 oz) soft white breadcrumbs
450 g (1 lb) seeded raisins
675 g (1 lb 8 oz) mixed peel
250 g (9 oz) currants
125 g (4 ½ oz) chopped dates
50 g (2 oz) blanched almonds
50 g (2 oz) chopped walnuts
75 ml (3 fl oz) brandy
125 ml (4 ½ fl oz) milk

G REASE two large ovenproof basins lightly with butter and
line with buttered baking parchment. Sift the flour with
the salt and mixed spice.

Beat the butter and sugar until creamy, light and fluffy. Add
the eggs one at a time, beating very well after each one is added.
Gently fold in the sifted flour. Add the breadcrumbs, fruit and
nuts, combine well. Mix in the brandy and milk making sure the

mixture is well blended. Pour the mixture equally into the two basins. They should be two-thirds full. Cover each mixture with a double layer of greased baking parchment and each bowl with a double layer of foil. Tie securely in place around the rim with string. Place the puddings in large pots of boiling water (the water should reach halfway up the sides of the basins).

Boil for four hours. Replace water as necessary with more boiling water. When cold, store in a cool dry place. Boil for a further two hours the day the pudding is used.

## BRANDY BUTTER

*125 g (4 ½ oz) butter*
*125 g (4 ½ oz) brown sugar*
*1 tablespoon brandy or to taste*

Beat the butter and sugar until creamy, light and fluffy. Add the brandy a little at a time, blending well. Chill.

*Always store Christmas pudding in a cool, dark, dry place to prevent it becoming mouldy and to allow it to mature.*

## CONFECTIONERS' CUSTARD

*250 ml (8 fl oz) cream (single)*
*250 ml (8 fl oz) milk*
*150 g (5 oz) caster (superfine) sugar*
*75 ml (3 fl oz) milk, extra*
*100 ml (4 fl oz) cream (single), extra*
*75 g (3 oz) cornflour (corn starch)*
*3 eggs, lightly beaten*

*4 level teaspoons gelatine*
*35 ml (1 ½ fl oz) water*

C OMBINE the cream, milk and sugar in a saucepan and bring to the boil. Remove from the heat. Mix together the extra milk, extra cream, cornflour and eggs. Pour the hot mixture over the cold mixture, stirring all the time. Cook over a medium heat until the custard boils and thickens, stirring all the time.

Sprinkle the gelatine over the water in a small bowl and soak for 5 to 10 minutes until softened. Stand in a pan of hot water until the gelatine has dissolved. Stir the water and gelatine into the hot custard. Use as required. Makes 900 ml (32 fl oz) of custard.

## CREME CARAMEL

*225 g (8 oz) sugar*
*4 tablespoons water*
*juice of 1 lemon*
*3 eggs*
*pinch of salt*
*2 tablespoons caster (superfine) sugar*
*600 ml (20 fl oz) milk*
*vanilla*

P REHEAT oven to 180 deg C (350 deg F). Heat sugar, water and lemon juice in a saucepan, stirring all the time until the sugar has dissolved. Boil without stirring until it forms a brown caramel liquid. Pour into an ungreased ovenproof dish or individual dishes and coat the sides and bottom with the caramel. Beat the eggs lightly with the sugar and salt. Stir in the milk and vanilla and pour into the prepared dish or dishes. Stand in a baking dish of water and bake until the custard has set. Turn out onto a serving dish.

## CUSTARD TART

*Sweet Biscuit Pastry*
*100 g (4 oz) butter*
*100 g (4 oz) caster (superfine) sugar*
*1 egg*
*225 g (8 oz) plain (all-purpose) flour*
*1 level teaspoon baking powder*

*Filling*
*3 eggs*
*2 tablespoons sugar*
*450 ml (15 fl oz) milk*
*½ teaspoon vanilla*
*nutmeg*

TO MAKE Sweet Biscuit Pastry: Sift the flour with the baking powder. Beat the butter and sugar until creamy, light and fluffy. Add the egg, beating very well. Add the flour and mix thoroughly. Knead to a smooth dough and refrigerate until required.

Preheat oven to 160 deg C (325 deg F). Grease a pie dish lightly with butter. Roll out pastry to 4 mm (⅛ in) thick. Place on the prepared dish and press into the shape of the dish. Cut off excess pastry and flute the edge.

# BIRD'S CUSTARD

BIRD'S CUSTARD AND JELLIES

To make Filling: Beat the eggs and sugar until creamy, light and fluffy. Add the milk and vanilla. Pour into the pastry. Sprinkle with nutmeg. Bake for 30 to 35 minutes or until custard has set.

## DATE PUDDING

*200 g (7 oz) plain (all-purpose) flour*
*2 level teaspoons baking powder*
*125 g (4 ½ oz) sugar*
*50 g (2 oz) butter*
*1 egg yolk*
*½ green cooking apple, peeled, cored and grated*
*100g (4 oz) dates, chopped*
*100 g (4 oz) walnuts, finely chopped (optional)*
*1 tablespoon instant coffee dissolved in 5 tablespoons water*
*1 egg white*

PREHEAT oven to 180 deg C (350 deg F). Grease individual ovenproof dishes with butter. Line bases with baking parchment. Sift flour with baking powder. Beat sugar and butter until creamy, light and fluffy. Add the egg yolk beating very well. Mix in the grated apple, dates and walnuts. Gently fold in the flour and coffee. Beat egg white until stiff peaks form and fold into mixture. Pour into prepared dishes. Place in a baking dish of water and bake for 25 to 30 minutes.

## FRITTERS

*100 g (4 oz) plain (all-purpose) flour*
*¼ level teaspoon salt*
*1 tablespoon melted butter*
*1 egg, separated*
*6 tablespoons warm water*
*1 egg white*
*oil for frying*
*fruit eg. whole bananas, pineapple rings etc.*

S IFT THE flour and salt. In a separate bowl mix the melted butter and the warm water with the egg yolk. Make a well in the centre of the flour and pour in the wet ingredients. Gradually stir the flour into the liquid until smooth. Beat the egg white until it forms stiff peaks then fold it into the mixture.

Add the fruit. Heat plenty of oil in a deep pan until hot. Using tongs or forks take batter-covered fruit out of bowl and immediately place in pan.

Deep fry in hot oil until fritters are a deep golden brown, about 3 minutes. Drain on kitchen paper and serve hot with ice cream or cream.

*Place a few drops of fritter batter into the hot oil to check that it is hot enough. If it sizzles and the batter quickly rises to the surface, the oil is at the correct temperature. Immediately drain fritters on kitchen or brown paper, dust with icing or caster sugar and serve at once.*

### APPLE FRITTERS

Add 1 level tablespoon sugar to batter. Peel, core and slice 2 large green cooking apples into rings. Dip in batter and fry.

### BANANA FRITTERS

Dip 4 to 6 whole bananas or bananas that have been split in half into the batter and fry.

## FRUIT CRUMBLE

*fresh fruit eg. apples*
*1 tablespoon sugar*
*150 g (5 oz) plain (all-purpose) flour*
*100 g (4 oz) brown sugar*
*100 g (4 oz) butter*

P REHEAT oven to 180 deg C (350 deg F). Grease an ovenproof dish or pie dish generously with butter.

Any fruit can be used that bakes well, such as peaches, apricots or apples. Peel and slice enough fruit to thickly cover the base of the pan. Sprinkle with sugar. Sift the flour. Stir together the flour and sugar. Rub the butter into the flour and sugar until it resembles breadcrumbs. Sprinkle thickly over the fruit. Bake for 40 minutes or until light golden brown.

## FRUIT JELLIES

---

*1 tablespoon gelatine*
*1 small teaspoon citric acid*
*250 g (9 oz) sugar*
*500 ml (17 fl oz) fruit juice*

---

M IX GELATINE, citric acid and sugar in a small basin. Boil fruit juice and pour into the mixture. Stir well to dissolve gelatine. Chill until set. Always add citric acid to fruit jellies.

## FRUIT SALAD

---

*3 bananas*
*1 pineapple*
*6 apricots*
*3 peaches*
*2 oranges*
*2 pears*
*2 apples*
*6 passionfruit*
*orange juice, freshly squeezed*
*cream, whipped*
*caster (superfine) sugar*

---

P EEL ALL the fruit and cut into small cubes. Place the fruit in layers into a glass bowl. Squeeze a little orange juice over each layer to stop it from discolouring and sprinkle with sugar. Oranges are best to have on top as they don't discolour. Decorate with whipped cream. Sprinkle with a little sugar. Serve with cream, ice cream or custard sauce.

## FRUIT SALAD JELLY

*½ orange*
*1 banana*
*1 slice pineapple*
*1 passionfruit*
*1 tablespoon sugar*
*1 packet jelly crystals*

C UT THE fruit into very small pieces and spread over a large shallow dish. Sprinkle with sugar. Dissolve the jelly crystals and pour over the fruit. Leave to set. When set, use a fork to break the jelly into small chunks. Serve with whipped cream, ice cream or custard sauce.

## GOLDEN DUMPLINGS

---

*250 g (9 oz) plain (all-purpose) flour*
*2 level teaspoons baking powder*
*3 dessertspoons butter*
*9 tablespoons milk*
*500 ml (17 fl oz) water*
*700 g (1 lb 10 oz) golden (light corn) syrup*

---

S IFT THE flour and the baking powder. Rub the butter into the sifted flour. Add enough milk to make a soft dough. Place the dough on a lightly floured board and knead lightly until smooth. Divide the dough into 12 equal portions. Roll into balls.

In a large saucepan combine the water and golden syrup. Heat until boiling, stirring all the time. Drop in the balls of dough and cover the saucepan tightly. Cook over a moderate heat for 20 minutes. Serve dumplings covered in the golden syrup sauce they were cooked in.

*When wanting jelly to set in a short time, pour half*
*the boiling water onto the crystals; stir until dissolved, then add*
*cold water for the other half of the required water.*

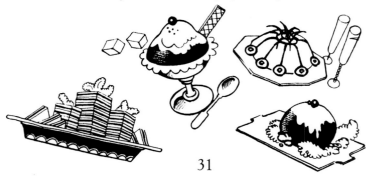

31

## JAM ROLY POLY

*185 g (6 ½ oz) plain (all-purpose) flour*
*2 level teaspoons baking powder*
*¼ teaspoon salt*
*1 rounded tablespoon butter*
*1 slightly rounded tablespoon sugar*
*1 egg*
*75 ml (3 fl oz) milk*
*jam*

*Syrup*
*175 g (6 oz) sugar*
*50 g (2 oz) butter*
*250 ml (8 fl oz) very hot water*

PREHEAT oven to 180 deg C (350 deg F). Grease a shallow ovenproof dish lightly with butter. Sift the flour with the baking powder and salt.

Rub the butter into the flour. Stir in the sugar. Thoroughly beat together the egg and milk. Make a well in the centre of the flour and pour the egg mixture into it. Gradually stir the flour into the liquid making a soft dough. Lightly knead dough until smooth.

Roll out to an oblong shape. Spread jam over the dough to within 14 mm (½ in) of the edges. Roll up like a Swiss (jelly) roll. Place in the prepared dish with the roll end underneath. Combine all the ingredients for the syrup and stir until the sugar has dissolved. Pour syrup over the roll. Bake for 45 minutes, basting occasionally with syrup. Serve hot with custard sauce or ice cream.

## LEMON CHIFFON PIE

*125 g (4 ½ oz) sweet biscuit crumbs*
*60 g (2 ½ oz) butter, melted*
*250 g (9 oz) sugar*
*250 ml (8 fl oz) water*
*2 eggs, separated*
*1 tablespoon gelatine, dissolved in a little hot water*
*juice of 2 lemons*
*grated rind of 1 lemon*

G REASE a 20 cm (8 in) springform pan lightly with butter. Combine biscuit crumbs and butter and press in the bottom of the pan to form a base. Refrigerate.

Combine sugar and water in a saucepan and heat gently,

33

stirring to dissolve the sugar. Add egg yolks, and stir until it thickens. Do not boil. Remove from heat and add gelatine. When cool stir in lemon juice and rind. Beat egg whites until stiff peaks form and fold into mixture. Pour into prepared pan and refrigerate.

*Heat a lemon thoroughly before squeezing,
and you will obtain nearly double
the amount of juice.*

## LEMON DELICIOUS

2 tablespoons plain (all-purpose) flour
1 tablespoon butter
185 g (6 ½ oz) sugar
2 eggs, separated
325 ml (11 fl oz) milk
juice of 2 lemons
grated rind of 1 lemon

P REHEAT oven to 160 deg C (325 deg F). Grease an ovenproof dish generously with butter.

Cream the butter and sugar until creamy, light and fluffy. Add the egg yolks one at a time, beating very well after each one is added. Sift the flour into the mixture and gently fold through, then stir in the milk. Add the lemon juice and rind and mix thoroughly. Beat the egg whites until stiff peaks form and fold into the mixture.

Pour the mixture into the prepared dish. Place the dish in baking dish of water and bake for 45 minutes or until set and light brown.

Hot Water magic
by RHEEM

## You need Hot Water 35 times a day...

We've proved it. For washing up, for washing down, for washing clothes and personal use, the average Australian family needs hot water at least 35 times every day.

With a Rheem Water Heating unit in your home, there's a constant reservoir of *hot* water —on tap—24 hours out of 24.

*Ask the 'men who know'. Master plumbers, architects, builders, electrical dealers, all will tell you it's the precision built unit that won't let you down.*

## RHEEM

### Automatic Hot Water-Storage Systems

*Particulars from Gas Companies, Electricity undertakings, Electrical Dealers and Hardware Merchants.*

## LEMON DUMPLINGS

*250 g (9 oz) plain (all-purpose) flour*
*2 level teaspoons baking powder*
*3 dessertspoons butter*
*9 tablespoons milk*
*750 ml (25 fl oz) water*
*225 g (8 oz) sugar*
*2 tablespoons golden (light corn) syrup*
*Juice of 2 lemons*

S IFT THE flour with the baking powder. Rub the butter into the sifted flour. Add enough milk to make a soft dough. Place the dough on a lightly floured board and knead lightly until smooth. Divide the dough into 12 equal portions. Roll into balls.

In a large saucepan combine the water, sugar, golden syrup and lemon juice. Heat until boiling, stirring all the time. Drop in the balls of dough and cover the saucepan tightly. Cook over a moderate heat for 20 minutes. Serve dumplings covered in the lemon sauce they were cooked in.

## LEMON MERINGUE PIE

*1 quantity rich shortcrust pastry (see Rich*
*Shortcrust Pastry recipe)*
*3 level tablespoons cornflour (cornstarch)*
*pinch of salt*
*185 g (6 ½ oz) sugar*
*325 ml (11 fl oz) water*
*3 egg yolks*
*4 tablespoons lemon juice*
*1 teaspoon grated lemon rind*
*60 g (2 ½ oz) butter*
*3 egg whites*
*125 g (4 ½ oz) caster (superfine) sugar*
*sifted icing sugar*

P REHEAT oven to 190 deg C (375 deg F). Lightly grease with butter a 20 cm (8 in) pie dish. Roll out pastry to fit pie dish. Prick the pastry all over with a fork. Line the pastry with baking parchment and fill with dried beans to bake the pie case blind. Bake for 15 minutes then for the next 10 minutes remove the paper and beans to allow the pastry to cook through. Cool.

To make the filling, combine the cornflour, salt and sugar in a saucepan and mix in the water. Stir over a moderate heat until

37

the mixture boils and thickens. Lower the heat and cook for 5 minutes, stirring occasionally. Remove from heat.

Beat the egg yolks, lemon juice and rind together. Pour into the cornflour mixture and gently heat for 2 minutes, stirring all the time. Beat in the butter until it is incorporated. Pour the mixture into the prepared pastry shell. Beat the egg whites until stiff peaks form. Gradually add the caster sugar. Beat until the sugar dissolves. Pour beaten egg white mixture over the filling and dust with icing sugar. Bake for 10 minutes or until lightly browned. Cool before serving.

## LEMON MOUSSE

---

*3 eggs, separated*
*2 tablespoons sugar*
*grated rind of half a lemon*
*juice of 1 lemon*
*15 g ( ½ oz) gelatine*
*2 tablespoons water*

---

B EAT THE egg yolks and sugar until light and creamy; add the lemon rind and juice. Dissolve the gelatine in the water

over a gentle heat. Mix into the egg mixture thoroughly. Beat the egg whites until soft peaks form and fold into the mixture. Pour into a glass dish and refrigerate until set. Decorate with sweetened whipped cream.

## PANCAKES

*100 g (4 oz) plain (all-purpose) flour*
*¼ level teaspoon salt*
*1 egg*
*250 ml (8 oz) milk*
*butter*

S IFT THE flour and salt. Beat the egg with about two-thirds of the milk. Make a well in the centre of the flour and pour the egg mixture into it. Gradually stir the flour into the liquid. Beat until smooth and light, about 5 minutes. Stir in the remainder of the milk. Stand for 1 hour. Pour into a jug.

Melt enough butter in a frying pan to grease it thickly. Pour in just enough batter to thinly cover the pan. Cook over a medium heat until the pancake is golden brown underneath, loosening the edges as it cooks. Turn the pancake over to cook the other side. Serve hot, freshly cooked. Makes about 5 pancakes.

### JAM PANCAKES

Spread hot pancake with jam and roll up. Dust top with sugar and cinnamon.

## LEMON PANCAKES

Sprinkle hot pancake with sugar and squeeze lemon juice over the sugar. Roll up.

## FRENCH CRÊPE SUZETTES

Add grated rind of an orange or lemon to the mixture. Cook the pancakes wafer thin. Fold in half and then in quarters. Pour over a hot sauce of 75 ml (3 fl oz) each of orange and lemon juice, sugar and melted butter.

## PASSIONFRUIT FLUMMERY

*325 g (11 ½ oz) sugar*
*125 ml (4 ½ fl oz) water*
*2 dessertspoons cornflour (cornstarch)*
*1 ¼ tablespoons gelatine*
*125 ml (4 ½ fl oz) hot water, extra*
*juice of 1 orange*
*juice of 1 lemon*
*pulp of 8 passionfruit*

COMBINE sugar and water in a saucepan and heat gently, stirring to dissolve the sugar. Thicken with cornflour mixed to a paste with a little water. Remove from heat. Dissolve gelatine in hot water and stir into the mixture. Add orange juice, lemon juice and passionfruit pulp. Leave to cool until it begins to set. Beat vigorously until frothy. Pour into a glass bowl and refrigerate.

## PAVLOVA

*4 egg whites*
*pinch of salt*
*250 g (9 oz) caster (superfine) sugar*
*1 dessertspoon cornflour (cornstarch)*
*1 teaspoon vinegar*
*1 teaspoon vanilla*

PREHEAT oven to 180 deg C (350 deg F). Grease a baking tray (sheet) lightly with butter. Draw a 20 cm (8 in) circle on a sheet of baking parchment. Grease the baking parchment lightly with butter and place on the tray (sheet). Beat egg whites and salt until stiff peaks form. Vigorously beat in sugar a little at a time, until sugar has dissolved.

Sprinkle over cornflour, vinegar and vanilla essence and fold in lightly. Mound onto the circle drawn on the prepared baking parchment.

Place in preheated oven and reduce heat to 150 deg C (300 deg F), and cook for 1 ¼ hours. Turn off oven and leave pavlova to cool. When cool decorate with whipped cream and fresh fruit.

*To keep an unbroken yolk of an egg,*
*cover with water.*

## QUEEN OF PUDDINGS

*500 ml (17 fl oz) milk, heated*
*125 g (4 ½ oz) fresh white breadcrumbs*
*2 eggs, separated*
*1 tablespoons sugar*
*2 teaspoons butter*
*1 teaspoon vanilla*
*1 tablespoon raspberry or other jam*
*pinch of salt*
*2 tablespoons caster (superfine) sugar*

P REHEAT oven to 180 deg C (350 deg F). Grease an ovenproof dish lightly with butter. Heat the milk and pour it over the breadcrumbs. Leave aside for about 30 minutes for the bread to swell. Thoroughly beat the egg yolks with the sugar, butter and vanilla. Add to breadcrumb mixture and beat until smooth.

Pour mixture into the prepared dish. Bake for 45 minutes or until set. Cool slightly.

Spread a thick layer of jam on the top, heating the jam if necessary, so that it will spread easily. Beat the egg whites until stiff peaks form. Gradually beat in the caster sugar. Pile beaten egg whites on top of the pudding. Sprinkle with the remaining sugar. Bake for a further 20 to 30 minutes or until the meringue has set. Serve hot.

## RASPBERRY ICE

800 g (1 lb 12 oz) raspberries
250 g (9 oz) sugar
500 ml (17 fl oz) water
juice of 1 orange
juice of 1 lemon
2 tablespoons grated orange rind

COMBINE raspberries, sugar and water in a saucepan and cook gently for 10 minutes. Add fruit juices and grated orange rind. Pour into a dish and freeze. Remove when frozen and break up and beat until fluffy. Return to dish and finish freezing.

## RICE PUDDING

*1 litre (34 fl oz) milk*
*125 g (4 ½ oz) sugar*
*125 g (4 ½ oz) rice, short-grain*
*2 tablespoons butter*
*½ teaspoon salt*
*½ teaspoon nutmeg*
*1 teaspoon vanilla*
*75 g (3 oz) sultanas (golden raisins) or raisins*
*75 ml (3 fl oz) cream (single)*

PREHEAT oven to 160 deg C (325 deg F). Have ready a pie or ovenproof dish Heat the milk until it is hot. Mix in the sugar, rice, butter, salt, nutmeg and vanilla. Pour into the prepared dish. Bake, uncovered, stirring often, for 2 hours. Stir in the sultanas or raisins. Pour over the cream. Bake for a further 30 minutes.

*To use a vanilla bean instead of vanilla*
*flavouring, steep the bean in warm milk for a few minutes*
*then remove. Wash and dry the bean so it can be used again.*
*Store the vanilla bean in an airtight jar containing*
*caster sugar and while the sugar preserves the bean it*
*takes up its perfume at the same time.*

45

## RICH SHORTCRUST PASTRY

*250 g (9 oz) plain (all-purpose) flour*
*pinch of salt*
*185 g (6 ½ oz) butter*
*1 tablespoon caster (superfine) sugar*
*1 egg yolk*
*1 ½ tablespoons water*

P REHEAT oven to 190 deg C (375 deg F). Sift the flour and salt into a large bowl. Rub the butter into the flour until it resembles breadcrumbs. Add the sugar. Beat together the egg yolk and the water. Make a well in the centre of the flour and pour in the egg mixture. Quickly mix to a firm dough. Knead lightly until it is smooth, then roll into a ball and chill for 30 minutes. Use as required.

## RHUBARB AND APPLE PIE

*250 g (9 oz) rich shortcrust pastry (see Rich*
*Shortcrust Pastry recipe)*
*500 g (1 lb 1 oz) green cooking apples, peeled, cored and sliced*
*1 bunch rhubarb, cut in 3.5 cm (1 ½ in) lengths*
*grated rind of 1 orange*
*3 tablespoons sugar*
*1 tablespoon caster (superfine) sugar for pie crust*

P REHEAT oven to 190 deg C (375 deg F). Generously grease a 25 cm (10 in) pie dish with butter. Mix in a bowl the sliced apple, rhubarb, orange rind and sugar. Spoon into the prepared dish. Roll out pastry on a lightly floured surface. Cut off a 1 cm

(½ in) strip and press around the rim of the pie dish. Brush with a little water. Lay the remaining pastry over the dish. Trim off excess pastry and crimp the edges. With any left over pieces of pastry make leaf shapes to decorate pie top. Brush with beaten egg white to glaze. Make two or three steam vents and sprinkle lightly with sugar. Bake for 30 minutes.

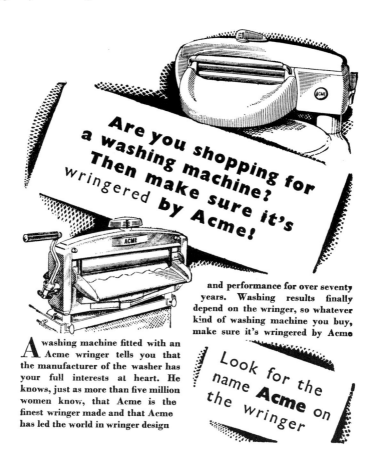

## RHUBARB FOOL

*185 g (6 ½ oz) sugar*
*250 ml (8 fl oz) water*
*1 bunch rhubarb, cut in 3.5 cm (1 ½ in) lengths*
*4 green cooking apples, peeled, cored and sliced*
*250 ml (8 fl oz) cream, lightly whipped*
*125 ml (4 ½ fl oz) milk*
*2 egg yolks*
*1 teaspoon arrowroot*
*3 tablespoons caster (superfine) sugar*
*vanilla*

COMBINE the sugar and the water in a saucepan and bring to the boil. Boil for 5 minutes. Add the rhubarb and apple and cook until soft. Remove from the syrup and purée in a processor. Chill in the refrigerator. Gently heat the milk. Beat the egg yolks, sugar and arrowroot until thick and light. Stir into the hot milk. Add vanilla. Gently heat the mixture, stirring all the time. When the custard coats the back of the spoon, remove from the heat and chill. Stir the custard into the fruit purée and gently fold in the cream, leaving the mixture slightly marbled. Spoon into individual glass dishes. Chill until ready to serve.

OVE
IOC
VARIET

## Sago Plum Pudding

375 ml (13 fl oz) milk
125 g (4 ½ oz) soft white breadcrumbs
4 tablespoons sago
100 g (4 oz) butter
250 g (9 oz) sugar
325 g (11 ½ oz) mixed fruit
2 tablespoons mixed peel, chopped
½ teaspoon nutmeg
¾ level teaspoon bicarbonate of soda (baking soda)
dissolved in 1 teaspoon cold water
2 eggs

G REASE an ovenproof bowl lightly with butter. Heat the milk and pour it over the breadcrumbs. Mix in the sago and butter and leave aside for about 30 minutes for the bread and sago to swell.

Add the sugar, fruit, nutmeg and bicarbonate of soda. Beat the eggs and stir into the mixture lightly, but thoroughly. Pour into the prepared bowl. It should two-thirds fill the basin. Cover the top of the mixture with a sheet of buttered baking parch-

ment. Then cover the top of the bowl with foil and secure with a piece of string around the rim of the bowl. Put into a large pot of boiling water. The water should reach half-way up the side of the bowl. Steam for 3 ½ hours. Individual dishes would take only 1 ½ hours.

## SAUCES

### CUSTARD SAUCE

*2 egg yolks*
*1 tablespoon sugar*
*300 ml (10 fl oz) milk*
*vanilla*

B EAT THE egg yolks and sugar lightly in a bowl. Warm the milk and beat into the egg yolks. Place the bowl over a saucepan of hot water or pour the mixture into a double boiler. Stirring all the time, cook until custard thickens about 20 minutes. It should coat the back of a spoon. Stir in vanilla.

### HOT CHOCOLATE SAUCE

*35 g (1 ½ oz) grated chocolate*
*1 tablespoon butter*
*125 ml (4 ½ fl oz) boiling water*
*1 tablespoon arrowroot*
*250 g (9 oz) sugar*
*½ teaspoon vanilla*

M ELT chocolate in a bowl placed over hot water or in a double boiler. Add the butter and boiling water. Mix in the arrowroot and sugar, stirring continuously. Boil for 3 minutes. Cool and add vanilla. Store in the refrigerator. May be served cold or heated before serving.

## SELF-SAUCING CHOCOLATE PUDDING

*115 g (4 ¼ oz) plain (all-purpose) flour*
*2 teaspoons baking powder*
*4 tablespoons cocoa powder*
*60 g (2 ½ oz) sugar*
*¼ teaspoon salt*
*125 ml (4 ½ fl oz) milk*
*2 tablespoons butter, melted*
*½ teaspoon vanilla*
*175 g (6 oz) brown sugar*
*250 ml (8 fl oz) boiling water*

PREHEAT oven to 180 deg C (350 deg F). Grease an ovenproof dish lightly with butter. Sift flour with baking powder, salt and 2 tablespoons of the cocoa powder. Stir in sugar. Mix in the milk, melted butter and vanilla, beating well. Pour mixture into the prepared dish. Combine brown sugar with remaining 2 tablespoons cocoa powder and sprinkle over mixture. Lastly, pour over boiling water. Bake for 40 to 45 minutes.

## SPOTTED DICK

225 g (8 oz) plain (all-purpose) flour
1 teaspoon baking powder
¼ teaspoon salt
100 g (4 oz) suet, finely chopped
75 g (3 oz) sugar
100 g (4 oz) currants
milk

GREASE a pudding cloth lightly with butter and dredge with flour. Sift the flour with the baking powder and salt. Mix in the suet, sugar and currants. Mix with enough milk to make a soft dough. Place the dough on the cloth. Leaving enough room for the pudding to swell, tie the pudding cloth ends together with a piece of string. Cook in fast boiling water for 2 hours. Add more boiling water if necessary.

## STEAMED PUDDING

*100 g (4 oz) plain (all-purpose) flour*
*¼ teaspoon baking powder*
*pinch of salt*
*100 g (4 oz) butter*
*100 g (4 oz) sugar*
*2 eggs*
*milk, if necessary*

G REASE an ovenproof bowl generously with butter. Sift the flour with the baking powder and salt.

Beat the butter and sugar until creamy, light and fluffy. Add the eggs one at a time, beating very well after each one is added.

Gently fold the sifted flour into the creamed mixture. Add milk, if required, to give a dropping consistency.

Spoon the mixture into the prepared bowl. It should two-thirds fill the bowl. Cover the top of the mixture with a sheet of buttered baking parchment. Then cover the top of the bowl with foil and secure with a piece of string around the rim of the bowl. Put into a large pot of boiling water. The water should reach halfway up the side of the bowl. Add extra boiling water if necessary. Steam for 1 ½ hours.

VARIATIONS ON STEAMED PUDDING

Syrup Pudding — Put 2 tablespoons of golden (light corn) syrup into the greased bowl before adding the pudding mixture.
Lemon or Orange — Add the finely grated rind of 1 lemon or orange after beating in the eggs.
Chocolate — Sieve 25 g (1 oz) cocoa powder into the dry ingredients, and add a little extra milk to mix.
Ginger — Add 50 g (2 oz) chopped preserved ginger to the dry ingredients.

STRUDEL

275 g (10 oz) plain (all-purpose) flour
pinch of salt
1 egg
1 tablespoon melted butter
225 ml (7 ½ fl oz) tepid water
melted butter, extra

Filling
3 large green cooking apples, peeled, cored and thinly sliced
100 g (4 oz) raisins
100 g (4 oz) walnuts, chopped
175 g (6 oz) sugar
1 teaspoon lemon rind
¼ teaspoon mixed spice

PREHEAT oven to 180 deg C (350 deg F). Grease a baking tray (sheet) lightly with butter. Sift the flour with the salt. In a separate bowl beat the egg and mix in the melted butter and

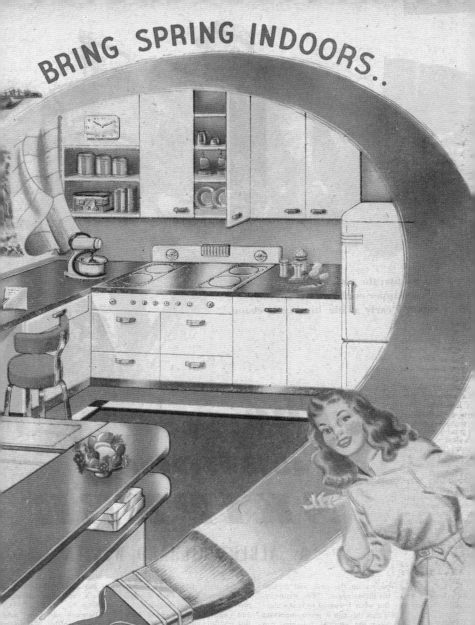

# BRING SPRING INDOORS..

OTHER STERLING QUALITY PRODUCTS:

ROOFRITE, PREPARED PAINT, PAVING PAINT, BATH ENAMEL,

RAYFLEX SYNTHETIC FINISH, SILVERGLOS, HOME TONE,

FLOOR STAINS, BRUSHING LACQUERS, LEATHERLAC, VARNISHES

warm water. Make a well in the centre of the flour and pour in the wet ingredients. Gradually stir the flour into the liquid until smooth. Flour your hands so the dough will not stick too much. Knead the dough until smooth and elastic. Cover and leave in a warm place for 1 hour.

Sprinkle a teatowel well with flour. Place dough in the centre of it and roll out slightly. Stretch the dough out by hand, working from the centre out, taking great care not to break the dough. It should be quite thin. Trim off any thick edges.

Prepare the filling by mixing together the apples, raisins, nuts, sugar, lemon rind and mixed spice. Brush the dough with some of the melted butter, sprinkle over the filling but not right to the edges. Pour over some more butter, then roll up the strudel, using the cloth to assist.

Place the strudel, sealed side down, on the prepared tray and bake for 40 minutes. If serving cool sprinkle with icing sugar.

*Pastry dough freezes very well if it has been packed in an airtight wrapper. The dough is best thawed in the refrigerator overnight. When making pastry in cooler weather you will need more liquid than in warmer months.*

## SUMMER PUDDING

---

*250 g (9 oz) apples, peeled, cored and sliced*
*500 g (17 oz) fresh or frozen raspberries*
*or blackberries*
*250 g (9 oz) sugar*
*stale white sliced bread,*
*with the crusts removed*

---

HAVE READY a bowl or pie dish. Place apples and raspberries or blackberries in a saucepan with the sugar. Heat gently until juices run from the fruit.

Line prepared dish with slices of overlapping bread to prevent juices escaping. Bread can be cut in fancy shapes or simply in triangles. Fill the lined pan with the fruit and cover the top with a layer of overlapping bread slices. Place a plate on top of the pudding. Put a heavy weight on the plate and refrigerate overnight. Turn out on to a serving dish.

## TAPIOCA CREAM

*100 g (4 oz) tapioca*
*water*
*1.2 litres (40 fl oz) milk*
*3 eggs, separated*
*3 tablespoons sugar*
*pinch of salt*
*vanilla*

SOAK tapioca overnight in water. Drain water from tapioca. Place tapioca and milk in a saucepan and simmer until tapioca is soft. Beat the egg yolks and sugar well and add to tapioca. Add salt. Boil gently for a few minutes stirring all the time, remove from heat and add vanilla. Beat egg whites until soft peaks form and fold into the mixture. Chill. Serve with stewed fruit.

## TRIFLE

*1 sponge cake or Swiss (jelly) roll*
*raspberry jam*
*3 macaroons*
*25 g (1 oz) almonds, chopped*
*75 ml (3 fl oz) fruit juice*
*125 ml (4 ½ fl oz) sherry or extra fruit juice*

*Custard*
*3 egg yolks*
*25 g (1 oz) caster (superfine) sugar*
*1 teaspoon cornflour*
*300 ml (10 fl oz) cream (double)*

*whipped cream*
*almonds, chopped (extra)*

HALVE sponge cake and spread with jam. Cut sponge cake or Swiss (jelly) roll in 1 cm (½ in) slices. Line a deep glass bowl with the slices. Sprinkle with macaroons and chopped almonds. Pour the fruit juice and sherry over the cake and let stand for 1 hour.

To make the custard, mix together the egg yolks, sugar and cornflour. Beat well. Heat the cream until hot but not boiling and pour over the egg mixture, beating all the time. Return the mixture to the saucepan and heat gently, stirring constantly. When the custard has thickened remove and allow to cool. Pour the custard over the top of the sponge cake and refrigerate until set. Decorate with whipped cream and chopped almonds. Serve with fruit salad or fruit salad jelly.

# ACKNOWLEDGEMENTS

With thanks to all the good friends who delved into their recipe collections, particularly Katrina Pizzini and her mother.

Also many thanks to the following companies for their help Arnott's Biscuits Limited, Cerebos Australia Ltd., Davis Gelatine (Aust) Co., Glynwed Australia, Kraft Foods Ltd., Letona Foods, Nestlé Australia Ltd., Rheem Australia Ltd., Southern Country Foods, Sunbeam Victa Corporation and Unifoods Pty. Ltd.